THE ROYAL COURT THEATRE
PRESENTS

The Sewing Group

Group

by E V Crowe

The Sewing Group was first performed at the Royal Court Jerwood
Theatre Upstairs, Sloane Square, on Thursday 10 November 2016.

The Sewing Group
by E V Crowe

CAST (in alphabetical order)

E **Nancy Crane**
C/Maggie **Fiona Glascott**
A **Jane Hazlegrove**
F and Mac **John Mackay**
B **Sarah Niles**
D/Sally **Alison O'Donnell**

Director & Designer **Stewart Laing**
Lighting Designer **Mike Brookes**
Sound Designer **Christopher Shutt**
Movement Director **Theo Clinkard**
Sewing Consultant **Ruth de Courcy**
Fight Director **Pamela Donald**
Assistant Director **Grace Gummer**
Casting Director **Amy Ball**
Production Manager **Matt Noddings**
Costume Supervisor **Natasha Ward**
Stage Managers **Nic Donithorn, Emma Tooze**
Stage Manager Work Placement **Daisy On**
Set Built by **Ridiculous Solutions**

The Royal Court & Stage Management wish to thank the following for their help with this production:
Axis Elevators Limited & Zahra Beswick.

The Sewing Group
by E V Crowe

E V Crowe **(Writer)**

For the Royal Court: **Hero, Kin, One Runs the Other Doesn't (Theatre Local)**.

Other theatre includes: **Brenda (HighTide/Yard); I Can Hear You (RSC); Liar Liar (Unicorn); Doris Day (Clean Break/Soho); Young Pretender (nabokov); ROTOR (Siobhan Davies Dance)**.

Television includes: **Glue, Big Girl**.

Radio includes: **How to Say Goodbye Properly**.

Awards include: **The Imison Award (How to Say Goodbye Properly)**.

E V Crowe was a member of the Royal Court Young Writers Programme. Her play Hero was part of the 2013 Olivier Award-Winning Season at the Jerwood Theatre Upstairs. Her play Kin was shortlisted for Charles Wintour Most Promising Playwright Award. She has been on attachment to the Royal Court Theatre, National Theatre Studio, Shauspiel Theatre, Frankfurt, and Helenico Theatre, Mexico City.

Mike Brookes **(Lighting Designer)**

As Lighting Designer, theatre includes: **Slope, An Argument About Sex, Paul Bright's Confessions of a Justified Sinner, The Salon Project (Untitled Projects); Eat Eat, Geneva, White Trash, Rantsoen, Butterfly, Grace, Susan & Darren, Old People Children & Animals, Make-Believe, Entitled, Summer Autumn Winter Spring (Quarantine)**.

Live & Public Arts projects include: **What if everything We Know Is Wrong?, Introduced Birdsong, The Perfect Human (And The Things We Do), 300 People & A Bear, Something Burning, Some Things Happen All At Once, Carrying Lyn/ Carrying Rubén, Just A little bit Of History Repeating, Grey line**.

Awards include: **Critic's Awards for Theatre in Scotland for Best Design with Stewart Laing & others (Confessions of a Justified Sinner); TMA/UK Theatre Award for Best Design (The Persians); Arts Council of Wales Creative Wales Award**.

Mike Brookes is an award-winning artist, director and designer whose live and public art works have been widely commissioned and presented internationally. Mike co-founded the performance collective Pearson/Brookes in 1997, where he most recently co-created The Persians (National Theatre Wales), Coriolan/us (NTW and RSC for London 2012) and ILIAD (NTW).

Theo Clinkard **(Movement Director)**

As Movement Director, theatre includes: **Ten Plagues (Traverse); The Complete Deaths (Spymonkey)**.

As Choreographer, dance includes: **Somewhat**

Still When Seen From Above (Tanztheater Wuppertal Pina Bausch); The Listening Room (Danza Contemporanea de Cuba); Bow & Arrow (Crysalis Dance, Galway); My Dance, Your Touch (Transitions Dance Company); We Become Panoramic (Verve); Wo/Man Made (S.E.A.D.).

Theo is a Brighton-based choreographer, performer and theatre designer who has worked regularly with Stewart Laing. Following twenty years performing with many of the UK's most celebrated choreographers, he formed his own seven-strong dance company in 2012. He has created Ordinary Courage, Chalk and Of Land & Tongue for the group and is currently planning This Bright Field, a work for twelve dancers that is due to premiere in 2017.

Nancy Crane **(E)**

For the Royal Court: **Now or Later, The Sweetest Swing in Baseball, Our Late Night, The Strip**.

Other theatre includes: **Teddy Ferrara (Donmar); Next Fall (Southwark Playhouse); Chimerica (Almeida/West End); Vieux Carre (King's Head); The Children's Hour (West End); Design for Living (Old Vic); Love the Sinner, Angels in America (National); Re-Orientations (Shanghai Dramatic Arts Centre); Dis-Orientations (Riverside); Chains of Dew, Trifles (Orange Tree); The Girl in the Goldfish Bowl, Six Degrees of Separation (Crucible, Sheffield); The Price (National Tour); Habitat (Royal Exchange, Manchester); A Wedding Story (National Tour)**;

Television includes: **Doctors, Nixon's The One, Upstairs Downstairs, Law & Order UK, The Special Relationship, Cambridge Spies, Strike Force**.

Film includes: **Leavey, Florence Foster Jenkins, The Danish Girl, Woman in Gold, Batman: The Dark Knight, The Road to Guantanamo, Sky Captain & the World of Tomorrow, The Machinist, The Fourth Protocol**.

Fiona Glascott **(C/Maggie)**

For the Royal Court: **Hitchcock Blonde (& West End)**.

Other theatre includes: **King Lear (Theatre Royal, Bath); Huis Clos (Trafalgar Studios); Kingdom of Earth (Print Room); Flea in her Ear (Old Vic); Here (Sky Arts); The Country Wife, Mahler's Conversation (West End); Whipping It Up (Bush); A Life (Abbey, Dublin); The Shaughraun (Royal Lyceum, Edinburgh); The Spirit of Annie Ross (Gate)**.

Television includes: **Episodes, Indian Summers, The Musketeers, Spooks, Miss Irena's Children, Clone, Foyle's War, Poirot, Jericho, The Long Firm, Omagh**.

Film includes: **Jadotville, Brooklyn, The Legend of Longwood, Emergo, The Deal, The Dual**.

Grace Gummer (Assistant Director)

As Director, for the Royal Court: **Sense, Theatre from the Windows, Theatre Uncontained, Stories from my Mother (Open Court).**

As Assistant Director, for the Royal Court: **We Anchor in Hope, Primetime 2016.**

As Director, other theatre includes: **BUTTER (Vaults); Liberator (503); Anonymous Anonymous (The Space); Dead Dove, Pineapple Juice (Brockley Jack).**

As Assosciate Director, other theatre includes: **Re:Home, Drawing Play (The Yard).**

As Assistant Director, other theatre includes: **Beyond Caring (National); Lines, Beyond Caring, Qudz (The Yard); Walking the Tightrope (Theatre Delicatessen).**

Grace is currently the Trainee Director at the Royal Court Theatre

Jane Hazlegrove (A)

For The Royal Court: **Harvest, Herons.**

Other theatre includes: **Mammals, Wishbones, Boom Bang-a-Bang, The Mortal Ash (Bush); Kes (Royal Exchange, Manchester); Holes in the Skin (Chichester Festival); The Accrington Pals (West Yorkshire Playhouse); Sing Yer Heart Out For The Lads (National); Snake in the Grass (Old Vic); The Wolves (Paines Plough).**

Television includes: **Casualty, Will, Faith, The Inspector Lynley Mysteries, Buried, Silent Witness, People Like Us, Without Motive, Hero to Zero, The Cops, Dinnerladies, Jonathan Creek, A Touch Of Frost, Making Out, Screen Two: Lovebirds, Shooting Stars, Threads.**

Film includes: **Cheeky, Heidi, The Whipping Boy.**

Stewart Laing (Director & Designer)

As Designer, for the Royal Court: **Waiting Room Germany, Holy Mothers.**

As Director, other theatre includes: **Home: Stornoway (National Theatre of Scotland); Ten Plagues (Traverse); The Maids (Citizens, Glasgow); Ophelia (Òran Mór); Titus Andronicus (Dundee Rep).**

Opera includes: **La Bohème (Scottish Opera); The Breasts of Tiresias, L'heure Espagnole (Grange Park Opera); Tosca (Norrlandsoperan); Dead Man Walking (Malmö Opera).**

Stewart is Artistic Director of Untitled Projects where his work includes J.G. Ballard Project, blind_sight, Slope, An Argument About Sex, The Salon Project, Paul Bright's Confessions of a Justified Sinner & Slope Redux.

John Mackay (F and Mac)

Theatre includes: **Wild, Drawing the Line, 55 Days (Hampstead); Measure for Measure (Young Vic); Oresteia (Almeida); Richard III, (Shakespeare at The Tobacco Factory); Going Dark (Young Vic/Sound & Fury); Little Eagles,** Antony & Cleopatra, King Lear, The Winter's Tale, Julius Caesar, The Grainstore, The Histories, Twelfth Night, As You Like It, Pilate, Hamlet (RSC); Six Characters in Search of an Author (Headlong/West End); Dark Earth (Traverse).

Television includes: **Hollow Crown II, The Honourable Woman, Holby City, Law & Order, The Great Transatlantic Cable, Doc Martin, Casualty, Trial & Retribution III.**

Sarah Niles (B)

For the Royal Court: **Father Comes Home From The Wars (Parts 1, 2 & 3), Truth & Reconciliation.**

Theatre includes: **Boy (Almeida); The Crucible (Old Vic); Anthony & Cleopatra (RSC/Off Broadway); Table, Mrs Affleck (National); A Question of Freedom (Feelgood); The Long Road (Curve, Leicester); The Quiet Little Englishman (Zho Visual); Play Size (ATC/Young Vic); Bones (Bush); The Bogus Woman, The Lion the Witch & the Wardrobe, To Kill a Mockingbird (Haymarket, Leicester); Entarete Musik (Amazonia Theatre Company); Lowdown High Notes (Red Ladder); Black Love (Black Arts Development Project); Caucasian Chalk Circle (Manchester Library).**

Television includes: **Marley's Ghosts, Lucky Man, My Baby, Catastrophe, Spotless, Death in Paradise, Waterloo Road, Being Human, Thorne: Sleepyhead, Beautiful People, Mister Eleven, Doctor Who, Peep Show, Touch of Frost.**

Film includes: **Still, Austenland, Cuban Fury, Now Is Good, London Boulevard, Games Men Play, Happy-Go-Lucky.**

Alison O'Donnell (D/Sally)

Theatre includes: **Much Ado About Nothing (The Faction); Brenda (HighTide/The Yard); Incognito (Bush/nabokov); Beached (Soho); White Rose (Firebrand); Boys (Soho/Headlong); Yerma (Gate/Hull Truck); The Hard Man (Scottish Theatres Consortium); My Romantic History (Bush/Crucible, Sheffield); Eigengrau (Bush); Dolls (National Theatre of Scotland); Lady Windermere's Fan (Òran Mór); The Assassination of Paris Hilton (Racked); Mad Funny Just (Creased); 2, 1 IN 5, (Hampstead Theatre Daring Pairings); Phaedre (Offstage); Barren (Old Vic New Voices); Broken Road (Hush Productions); Love Sex & Cider (Jacuzzi).**

Television includes: **Shetland, Holby City, Feel the Force.**

Christopher Shutt (Sound Designer)

For the Royal Court: **Escaped Alone, Love & Information (& New York), Kin, Aunt Dan & Lemon, Bliss, Free Outgoing, The Arsonists, Serious Money, Road.**

Other theatre includes: **The Winter's Tale, Romeo & Juliet, The Entertainer (West End); The Merchant of Venice (Globe); The Father (Theatre Royal, Bath/Tricycle/West End); Hamlet (Barbican); Bull (Young Vic); Here We Go, The Beaux' Stratagem, Man & Superman, The James Plays I & II, From Morning to**

Midnight, Strange Interlude, Timon of Athens, The Last of the Haussmans, The White Guard, Burnt by the Sun, Every Good Boy Deserves Favour, The Hour We Knew Nothing of Each Other, War Horse (& West End), Philistines, Happy Days, Thérèse Raquin, The Seagull, Burn/Chatroom/Citizenship, Coram Boy, A Dream Play, A Minute Too Late, Measure for Measure, Mourning Becomes Elektra, Play Without Words, Machinal (National); Faith Healer, Privacy, The Same Deep Water As Me, Philadelphia, Here I Come!, Piaf, The Man Who Had All the Luck, Hecuba (Donmar); The Playboy of the Western World, All About My Mother, Life x 3 (Old Vic); Ruined, Judgement Day (Almeida); Desire Under the Elms, Blasted (Lyric, Hammersmith); Wild, A Human Being Died That Night, And No More Shall We Part, For Once (Hampstead); Thyestes (Arcola); Shoes (Sadler's Wells); The Caretaker (Crucible, Sheffield/Tricycle); Julius Caesar (Barbican); Oppenheimer (& West End), The Two Gentlemen of Verona, Wendy & Peter Pan, Candide, Twelfth Night, The Comedy of Errors, The Tempest, King Lear, Romeo & Juliet, King John, Much Ado About Nothing (RSC); Macbeth (Manchester International Festival/ New York); Drum Belly (Abbey, Dublin); Crave/4:48 Psychosis (Sheffield Theatres); Far Away, A Midsummer Night's Dream (Bristol Old Vic); Good (Royal Exchange, Manchester); Man of Aran (Druid); Little Otik, The Bacchae (National Theatre of Scotland); Riders to the Sea (ENO); A Disappearing Number, The Elephant Vanishes, Mnemonic, The Noise of Time, The Street of Crocodiles, The Three Lives of Lucie Cabrol, The Caucasian Chalk Circle (Complicité); A Human Being Died That Night, Macbeth, All My Sons, The Resistible Rise of Arturo Ui, Happy Days, A Moon for the Misbegotten, Coram Boy, Humble Boy, Not About Nightingales, Mnemonic (Broadway).

Awards include: Tony Award for Best Sound Design of a Play (War Horse); Evening Standard Theatre Award for Best Play (A Disappearing Number); New York Drama Desk Awards for Outstanding Sound Design (Mnemonic, Not About Nightingales).

Natasha Ward (Costume Supervisor)

For the Royal Court: Human Animals, The Wolf from the Door.

Other theatre includes: A Streetcar Named Desire (Young Vic/St Ann's Warehouse, New York); The Inn at Lydda, The Winter's Tale (Globe); Outside Mulling (Ustinov, Bath); The King's Speech (Chichester Festival/Birmingham Rep/UK Tour); Hello Goodbye (Hampstead); The Colby Sisters, Bracken Moor, Paper Dolls (Tricycle); Handbagged, Bakersfield Mist, Privates on Parade, Henry V, View from the Bridge (West End), Translations (Crucible, Sheffield/ETT); Richard II, The Recruiting Officer (Donmar); Carrie's War (Sadler's Wells).

As Assistant/Associate Costume Supervisor: War Horse (UK Tour/West End); Sweet Charity (Menier Chocolate Factory/West End); Evita (European tour); La Cage Aux Folles (Broadway); Carrie's War (West End).

Natasha was the Assistant Costume Buyer at the National Theatre from 2010 to 2011.

THE ROYAL COURT THEATRE

The Royal Court Theatre is the writers' theatre. It is the leading force in world theatre for energetically cultivating writers – undiscovered, emerging and established.

Through the writers, the Royal Court is at the forefront of creating restless, alert, provocative theatre about now. We open our doors to the unheard voices and free thinkers that, through their writing, change our way of seeing.

Over 120,000 people visit the Royal Court in Sloane Square, London, each year and many thousands more see our work elsewhere through transfers to the West End and New York, UK and international tours, digital platforms, our residencies across London, and our site-specific work. Through all our work we strive to inspire audiences and influence future writers with radical thinking and provocative discussion.

The Royal Court's extensive development activity encompasses a diverse range of writers and artists and includes an ongoing programme of writers' attachments, readings, workshops and playwriting groups. Twenty years of the International Department's pioneering work around the world means the Royal Court has relationships with writers on every continent.

Within the past sixty years, John Osborne, Samuel Beckett, Arnold Wesker, Ann Jellicoe, Howard Brenton and David Hare have started their careers at the Court.

Many others including Caryl Churchill, Athol Fugard, Mark Ravenhill, Simon Stephens, debbie tucker green, Sarah Kane - and, more recently, Lucy Kirkwood, Nick Payne, Penelope Skinner and Alistair McDowall - have followed.

The Royal Court has produced many iconic plays from Laura Wade's **Posh** to Jez Butterworth's **Jerusalem** and Martin McDonagh's **Hangmen**.

Royal Court plays from every decade are now performed on stage and taught in classrooms and universities across the globe.

It is because of this commitment to the writer that we believe there is no more important theatre in the world than the Royal Court.

Supported using public funding by
ARTS COUNCIL ENGLAND

17 Nov – 14 Jan

THE CHILDREN
By Lucy Kirkwood

ROYAL

Tickets from £12

royalcourttheatre.com

Supported using public funding by
**ARTS COUNCIL
ENGLAND**

Sloane Square London, SW1W 8AS
🐦 royalcourt f royalcourttheatre
⊖ Sloane Square ⇄ Victoria Station

COURT

ROYAL COURT SUPPORTERS

The Royal Court is a registered charity and not-for-profit company. We need to raise £1.7 million every year in addition to our core grant from the Arts Council and our ticket income to achieve what we do.

We have significant and longstanding relationships with many generous organisations and individuals who provide vital support. Royal Court supporters enable us to remain the writers' theatre, find stories from everywhere and create theatre for everyone.

We can't do it without you.

The Genesis Foundation supports the Royal Court's work with International Playwrights. Bloomberg supports Beyond the Court. Jerwood Charitable Foundation supports emerging writers through the Jerwood New Playwrights series. The Pinter Commission is given annually by his widow, Lady Antonia Fraser, to support a new commission at the Royal Court.

PUBLIC FUNDING

Arts Council England, London
British Council

CHARITABLE DONATIONS

The Bryan Adams Charitable Trust
The Austin & Hope Pilkington Trust
Martin Bowley Charitable Trust
Gerald Chapman Fund
CHK Charities
The City Bridge Trust
The Clifford Chance Foundation
Cockayne - Grants for the Arts
The Ernest Cook Trust
Cowley Charitable Trust
The Dorset Foundation
The Eranda Rothschild Foundation
Lady Antonia Fraser for

The Pinter Commission
Genesis Foundation
The Golden Bottle Trust
The Haberdashers' Company
The Paul Hamlyn Foundation
Roderick & Elizabeth Jack
Jerwood Charitable Foundation
Kirsh Foundation
The Mackintosh Foundation
Marina Kleinwort Trust
The Andrew Lloyd Webber Foundation
The London Community Foundation
John Lyon's Charity
Clare McIntyre's Bursary
The Andrew W. Mellon Foundation
The Mercers' Company
The Portrack Charitable Trust
The David & Elaine Potter Foundation
The Richard Radcliffe Charitable Trust
Rose Foundation
Royal Victoria Hall Foundation
The Sackler Trust
The Sobell Foundation
John Thaw Foundation
The Vandervell Foundation
Sir Siegmund Warburg's Voluntary Settlement
The Garfield Weston Foundation
The Wolfson Foundation

CORPORATE SPONSORS

AlixPartners
Aqua Financial Solutions Ltd
Bloomberg
Colbert

Edwardian Hotels, London
Fever-Tree
Gedye & Sons
Kirkland & Ellis International LLP
Kudos
MAC

BUSINESS MEMBERS

Auerbach & Steele Opticians
CNC – Communications & Network Consulting
Cream
Hugo Boss UK
Lansons
Left Bank Pictures
Rockspring Property Investment Managers
Tetragon Financial Group
Vanity Fair

Supported using public funding by
ARTS COUNCIL ENGLAND

"There is no more important theatre in the world than the Royal Court."

– Simon Stephens

The Royal Court's mission has remained unchanged since George Devine founded the theatre in 1956. We continue to work with writers to put provocative and cutting edge work on our stages and, thanks to our Members and Supporters Circles, we are able to undertake the vital support of writers and develop their plays.

In acknowledgement of their support, our Supporters and Members become part of the Royal Court family with invitations to press nights and private events for our shows, exclusive insights to the plays at season launch lunches and the opportunity to celebrate with us at the Royal Court annual party.

Invest with us as we seek out, develop and nurture new voices together.

We can't do it without you.

Members and Supporters Circles

To join from £250 a year please contact:

Charlotte Cole, Development Officer
charlottecole@royalcourttheatre.com
020 7565 5049

The Sewing Group

E. V. Crowe's plays include *Kin* (Royal Court), *Hero* (Royal Court), *I Can Hear You* (RSC), *Brenda* (HighTide/ The Yard), *Young Pretender* (nabakov) and *Doris Day* (Clean Break/Soho).

by the same author
from Faber

KIN
HERO

E. V. CROWE

The Sewing Group

FABER & FABER

First published in 2016
by Faber and Faber Limited
74–77 Great Russell Street,
London WC1B 3DA

Typeset by Country Setting, Kingsdown, Kent CT14 8ES
Printed and bound by CPI Group (UK) Ltd, Croydon CR0 4YY

A CIP record for this book
is available from the British Library

ISBN 978-0-571-33477-3

2 4 6 8 10 9 7 5 3 1

For Erik

Acknowledgements

A number of actors improvised, discussed and read during the development of this play, and I would like to thank each of them, I could not have written this play without them: Claire Skinner, Geoffrey Streatfield, Shannon Tarbet, Romola Garai, Adetomiwa Edun, Adam Gillen, Bryony Hannah, Amanda Drew, Tobias Menzies, Annette Badland, Justine Mitchell, Hattie Morahan, Kate O'Flynn, Marion Bailey, Rory Keenan.

The play evolved from an initial research process and 'rough cut' in 2013 to eventually become *The Sewing Group*. I am grateful to those from industry I met as part of my research. My sincere thanks to Vicky Featherstone, Dominic Cooke, Carrie Cracknell, Emily Mcloughlin, Clare McQuillan, Giles Smart, Penny Skinner, Jess Sykes, Georgia Kanner, Dinah Wood, Steve King and in particular Stewart Laing and everyone at the Royal Court.

I would like to thank the audience in advance, for their imaginations.

The **Sewing Group** was first performed in the Jerwood Theatre Upstairs at the Royal Court Theatre, London, on 10 November 2016. The cast, in alphabetical order, was as follows:

E Nancy Crane
C / Maggie Fiona Glascott
A Jane Hazlegrove
F *and* **Mac** John Mackay
B Sarah Niles
D / Sally Alison O'Donnell

Director and Designer Stewart Laing
Lighting Designer Mike Brookes
Sound Designer Christopher Shutt

Characters

A
female

B
female

C / Maggie
female

D / Sally
female

E
female

F
male

Mac
male
played by same actor as F

A room made solely of untreated wood.

Five low, wooden stools.

THE SEWING GROUP

Someday in the future people will look back
and remember how beautiful it once was.

Jodie Foster, 2013

ONE

A and B in long, black dresses, suggestive of 1700s rural England.
    They look like a picture ripped out of a history book.
    Candlelight.
    They embroider on to a small piece of lace.
    A notable silence.
    A looks up at B.
    B glances back.
    They return to their work.

TWO

F and C watch A and B sew.

F She's come from the next village. To live with her aunt and uncle.

    A and B look at C.
    F goes, leaves C.
    C stands adrift, unsure where to put herself.
    Then sits.

THREE

They sew.

C What kind of crops do you farm?

    Pause.

What county is it?

Pause.

A The stitches, they catch if they get too big.

FOUR

They sew.
    C opens the little window.
    Sits.
    She swaps her stool for another.

B The cross-stitch!

    C tries to sew.

C What is it?

B Undergarments.

A The winter cometh! It, cometh!

C Is it cold here? Colder than out there?

    Pause.

What do you do *while* you're sewing?

    Silence.

A Sew.

FIVE

A, B and C sew.
    A hums.
    C smiles at her politely.
    They continue to sew.
    C stares right at A until she stops.

SIX

They sew.

B Would you rather work in the fields, dear?

A Or help your aunt in the kitchen?

C I don't know. No.

   Pause.

Is it really, really noisy or really, really quiet? I can't tell.

SEVEN

They sew.

C 'Aunt' and 'Uncle', they want me to be of use.

   Pause.

Sewing is –

A It's for making ends meet!

B For the good of.

A Mending also.

B Sewing is a craft.

   Pause.

A Did you sleep well last night?

C I'm confused now.

A How are you this morning?

C My mind's gone blank.

   They sew slowly.

EIGHT

A, B and C.
  They sew.

A Does she have a love interest?

C –

A We're only teasing.

B A little laugh.

  Pause.

C He's a stack. He's massive.

A A stack?

B Sewing is an exercise in self-development. Keep going and you'll strike at something!

C His name also rhymes with stack. He's called Mac.

They sew.

A Such neat rows!

B Thank you!

They sew.

A Look, the birds passing by!

B And blossom in through the open door.

She finds some on the floor and holds it out to C.
C inhales the smell.

A Don't you think it's nice?

ELEVEN

They sew.
   A fart.
   Unmistakably another.
   F comes in and leaves immediately.
   C covers her mouth with her sleeve, trying not to
inhale.
   A and B suppress laughter. Their bodies shake.
   C laughs so hard a tear runs down her cheek.

TWELVE

They sew.

B You choose the colour for the next section.

C Oh.

A We'd like you to.

   Pause.

C Once I start something, I . . . red.

A Red?

B OK. Red.

C Don't put me in charge!

THIRTEEN

They sew.

C Red.

A Red?

B OK. Red.

C And it needs to be a stronger design too. Double the detail.

A It will take us twice as long.

B At least! Our arms will ache.

   Pause.

C I can see how the pattern works now.

FOURTEEN

They sew.

C Big. Double the size.

A It will take us twice as long.

B At least! Our arms will fall off.

C I think more hands.

FIFTEEN

A, B and F.
   They sit in silence, thinking.

F OK.

SIXTEEN

A and B look at D.
  D ignores them.

C This is our red item.

D Fine.

A We can show you how to sew.

C It's like ones and noughts.

B Any questions you can ask us.

C I came up with it.

A Sewing?

C Doing it my way, my new way.

B It's the same.

C We're doing it my way though. Aren't we?

  A and B look at each other, unsure.

B Enthusiasm!

D Who leads?

A I usually –

C You're doing very well! Keep sewing a bit better along here!

B This one can be hers.

C I feel a bit more enthusiastic.

A Oh yes.

C Don't trample my enthusiasm.

B We're not.

A We won't.

C I'm very task-orientated.

D What colour?

C They did teal before.

They sew.

D Is it supposed to be wonky?

A Oh dear.

B Oh no.

C It's not, is it?

Pause.

It's because you're new.

D I didn't, did I?

A No!

B No.

C It's her end that's wonky.

A It's not so bad.

B It's not perfect on your part.

C But I decided the red and the double.

D Have I ruined it?

A –

C Forget it then.

A You don't have to do that.

B You don't have to go.

C She knows it's her.

D I said at the beginning I'm not a strong sewer.

D leaves.
Silence.

C Is anyone else actually quite thirsty?

SEVENTEEN

A and B sit, not sewing, C watches them.

A Hard to start.

B Where to start.

A Idle hands.

B She's so particular.

A Before we knew what we were doing.

B We just did it.

A Same as before.

B Oh dear.

A Oh dear.

B We've lost our thread.

A Ha ha.

B Ho hum.

A Only sewing.

B We're here.

A We're waiting.

B We're just –

A Double or single. Red or teal.

B What next.

A What did you say?

B I said 'what next'.

A That's what the feeling is.

B What next.

A Say it again.

B What next.

A That's the feeling.

B What next.

A What next.

B That's how she makes me feel.

   C enters as if out of breath from outside.

C She's missing!

A Oh dear.

C I've looked all over.

B Did you look by the river?

C Yes.

A By the church?

C Yes.

B Up in the fields?

C Yes.

A At her house?

C EVERYWHERE.

B She can't be far. She has six children.

A Six.

C Six? Really? Six?

B Six.

C What?

A Six?

C Well. OK.

B She's a part of the community.

C Big part.

D arrives.

You went missing.

D No I didn't.

C I think.

D I don't remember this bit.

EIGHTEEN

E watches C as she sews.

E I brought you some bread.

C Thank you.

E Eat.

C No gluten.

E What?

C Before.

E Oh.

C I'm gluten free.

C sighs, impatient.

You're my 'aunt', that's correct isn't it?

E Yes.

C What am I like?

E You're very pleasant and sweet.

C OK.

E And you can dance well and you say your prayers.

C OK.

E And you work in the fields too and you do an honest day's work every day.

C The sewing?

E Some women sew. You sew.

C It's hard work.

E You're healing.

C What am I healing?

E Body and soul.

C Did '*I*' do something 'bad'. Before I came here?

E –

C What did I do? Did I run away? Did I steal something? Was I? Did I . . .? What did I do wrong?

E Have you done something bad?

C I'm asking you. Have I?

   Pause.

Shouldn't I be talking to a man of the church?

E Um.

C I might prefer it.

E You'd rather talk to someone else?

Pause.

We think an honest day's work does a lot for a person.

C Really?

E Yes.

C Honest.

E Do your arms ache?

C A bit. Yes. Is that good?

E We think so.

C The stools.

E It is uncomfortable.

NINETEEN

A, B, C, D, E and F.

F She came to me at my parish.

C The church.

F Yes my parish at the church.

C And I said –

F She asked me about words.

A Our words?

B That's right.

F She asked that I make an announcement to the community that we no longer use some of the words that are commonplace amoung us.

A Which words?

F –

D She wants that we no longer say 'community', she asked that we don't say 'thread'.

A We have to say 'thread'.

B We need to say 'community'.

F I have spoken very clearly with her and I have told her that she is new here and that she must live how we live.

C And loop and pattern.

D Those words belong to us. Historically.

F And if she does not, she will have to leave.

D OK.

F We need to see something from her. We need to see something of the goodness of her soul.

> *Pause.*

C I'm participating.

F Good. Thank you.

> *A pats C's hand.*
> *C finds herself unable to respond.*
> *She withdraws her hand.*
> *C looks at F, impatient.*

C Maybe if something *more* were to happen? For the score.

> *Pause.*

F Like what?

TWENTY

A, B, C and D sewing quietly.
  C looks at D.

C She's crying.

B She's grieving.

A It's incredibly sad.

C What happened?

A Her husband passed.

  D looks around for F.

D Me?

TWENTY-ONE

A, B, C and D sewing quietly.
  D crying a bit.

C She's crying.

B She's grieving.

A It's sad.

B What happened?

C Her husband was killed by a runaway bullock.

B A bullock?

A Very sad.

B She's grieving.

A Yes.

C Oh no.

D stops crying altogether.

A We should do something to help.

TWENTY-TWO

A, B, C and D sewing quietly.
D crying.

C She's crying.

B She's grieving.

A It's sad.

C What happened?

B Her husband was killed by a runaway bullock.

C A bullock?

A Very sad.

C She's grieving?

A Yes.

C Are you OK?

D sobs more.
Pause.

C We should do something to help!

TWENTY-THREE

A and B wait.
C comes in with D who has a bundle of clothes.

D These are his things.

C We went to her house.

D holds up some men's trousers and a man's shirt.

These are his clothes. It's compelling. I need a knife.

> *A reluctantly passes C a pair of scissors.*
> *B looks at A.*
> *C sets the clothes on the ground.*
> *She cuts them into squares.*

D What are you doing?! It's all I have left of him. He was my husband.

TWENTY-FOUR

A, B, C and D gather.
> *D holds up the now half cut-up clothes. The scissors are on a stool.*

A Tell us, child.

C I want us to make a quilt of her husband's clothes. And then at night when she sleeps, she can have his arms around her. She can lie there, asleep, in his arms. In his embrace.

> *Silence.*

B Beautiful.

> *D eyes C suspiciously.*

C It will make her pain easier to bear. I feel her pain. What is must be like to lose your husband.

D He was my soulmate.

C Your soulmate?

D Yes.

C Interesting.

D Yes.

C Yes.

D Yes.

C OK.

D That's why I'm so sad.

C Your *soulmate*?

D I'm grieving.

C A quilt is a sort of blanket, made up of patches. In case.

TWENTY-FIVE

C and D gather.
  D holds up a perfect stack of patches made from the clothes. The scissors are on a stool.

D It's all I have of him.

  Pause.

C You don't actually have six kids? How many do you have?

D I can't . . . One. You?

C Two.

D They live round here?

C No. You?

D We all live . . . (*She mouths.*) West. Big family thing.

C You're all together?

D Shh. Yeah. Why?

TWENTY-SIX

A, B, C and D sew the quilt serenely.
  F enters.

F What joy to behold. Such tranquillity!

D We're making a quilt from my husband's clothes, so I can have his loving arms around me at night.

F Whose idea was this?

C Mine!

F What a dear invention.

C I know.

F Such high compassion, and human understanding.

C OK, thanks.

F Such investment in the emotional lives of others.

C Yes.

  Pause.

It's a right thing to do. Isn't it?

F It's . . . within.

TWENTY-SEVEN

C and D look at the finished quilt.

C What do you see?

D What joy!

C Yes.

D Joy in despair!

C You can tell so much about a person once their stuff is made into a quilt.

D Yes! This is where he tore his shirt, trying to save a child from the river.

C Yes.

D This is where a little blood leaked after a wound from chopping wood.

C Yes.

Pause.

And this?

D What?

C This?

D Um. I can't see.

C An ale stain maybe.

D Perhaps!

C From where he got so drunk he didn't know his own name. Didn't know where he lived.

D Um.

C And slept God knows where with God knows who.

D OK.

C And this, this is a jacket he stole from his father who had worked hard to earn it. Your husband took it.

D Yes.

C It's very moving to see a whole person's life up there. A very, average, very, normal person. So real-lifey.

D Well. Yes and well done.

C claps her hands together, pleased.

34

TWENTY-EIGHT

F and C sit together.

F When I first came to the . . .

C When I first came to the village what did you see?

F I saw a woman, a *young* woman, torn inside. An upset, a void.

C A very successful young woman.

F A darkness.

C Not so much a darkness.

F I felt that you have grown cold to the world.

C So?

F That you are busy in your own endeavours.

C Yep.

F And that you have forgotten what it is to be part of a community. To be part of village life and to take time to smell the blossom so to speak.

C Maybe.

F It can be hard to learn to sew.

C It's fiddly.

F And results are slow.

C It's pretty –

F But I have seen a change in you.

C Yes?

F I have seen a glimmer of true light shining from your soul. As if a wound is being healed.

C OK.

F Being part of any community is possible.

C Well.

F Yes.

C That's good then.

F Yes.

   C looks at the door, restless.

C I'm pretty busy.

F OK.

C OK.

F For those who have truly opened their hearts.

C It's not very different to my old life.

F And you're good at it.

C I am, aren't I?

F I mean the others report that you learn swiftly.

C I do.

F That you have progressed.

C Well, it's not that hard. Oxbridge.

F I meant here.

C Thank you.

F Thank you.

C So out of ten, how well did I do?

F –

C It is out of ten?

F We have enjoyed your presence and are pleased with the quilt, our scoring is deliberately simple . . . Five.

C –

F Six, maybe.

C I *sewed*.

F The community felt we enjoyed having you. But we perhaps didn't feel you really gave yourself to the project and you strayed a little from the agreed arc.

C Um.

F And here, I fear we must part. It has been a joy and an 'immersive experience'.

> *Sweeping, orchestral 'end of the journey' music starts.*

C You can't put me in the 1700s, I sew, then 'five'.

F I'm sorry you're disappointed.

> *C looks at her watch. They've finished early.*

C Honestly. I've been very polite, I've played along.

> *F looks up, is just about to raise his hand, a kind of signal. The lights flicker.*
> *C interjects, confident, aggressive.*

I've noticed something about you. (*Pause.*) I've observed that you don't always communicate well with your flock.

F What?

C I've noticed you sometimes st-st-stumble over your words, and that people really don't give you much authority.

F I love the good people here.

C Yes but you don't *know* them.

F I'm a simple man.

C You could be more adept.

F I know their souls.

C But wouldn't it be better to really get to know them?
So you know you can trust them?

F looks beyond the room into the lights.

F Do we have time?

TWENTY-NINE

A, B and D listen to C.

C Each one of us makes a quilt, about ourselves.

A I'll make yours.

B I'll make yours.

C Make your own. That's the point!

A That's not easy.

C Make a quilt using your own everyday clothes.

D What work do you do?

C It's the natural progression from your husband's quilt.

D But that was to help me grieve.

C Yes but we 'discovered' something interesting.

D Who is this for?

C It's the only course of action. One development leads
to the next. And so on and so forth into the future!

Pause.

They're for the church.

A Lovely.

B What a contribution.

C Uh-huh.

A We will feel so good.

B I'll want mine to be perfect.

C Yes, you must make a quilt that truly represents you.
So someone can look at it, and know it's you but also
learn things they didn't know about you.

They take out their patches. C takes one from B's pile.

It's fun. I can see who likes to sit on grass. You like to
walk alone, OK? And dream of cakes and warm milk,
OK?

She takes one of A's patches.

I can see you like to go and visit . . . babies, OK? (*She
smells it.*) You have a love so great for infants, OK?

And one from D.

There is a little patch here. This must be where your tears
have fallen so hard they have stained it, OK?
See how fascinating it is, see what we reveal about
ourselves? How wonderful and dear and unique we all
are? So fun. OK.

D considers C, suspicious.

D What's your job out there?

THIRTY

F is waiting. D watches. C carries in a pile of quilts.

C Everyone in the village is beyond excited. Soon we will
have quilts made by everyone, about themselves.

F What will we do with the quilts?

C You can hang them in the village hall and people can come and admire them, and better know each person in the village. Or when they get too many, a barn or somesuch.

F You have become such a dear.

C No, no.

F Truly, there is sunshine coming from your heart. Even the children?

C Especially the children. Their quilts will reveal not only who they are but who they might become. What darlings they might become.

F A true wonder.

Pause.

C And then. When something bad happens.

F It happens rarely here.

C *If* something bad happens. You're protected.

F We have the Lord.

C Yep but, if for example there is a theft.

F I've not seen it yet.

C No, but if there were.

F –

C Then you might be better able to identify who did it.

F I don't see how.

C Well, if everyone makes a quilt about themselves, you can go to the storage unit of quilts and look at them, and work out who stole the milk or whatever.

F I would just see quilts.

C OK then. you'll need someone like me. For example, to look at the quilts and tell you something about them that observes something about their specific behaviour, that links them to the crime.

I can see she likes to sit on grass. She searches for places to go to alone perhaps? Secret places. Maybe she hides things under a tree somewhere. A secret stash.

I can see she goes and visits babies. There is food on the shoulder part. She still wishes for another child. Let's hope she can be trusted not to steal one.

And from D.

There is already semen here from another man. She grieves fast maybe!? Maybe we don't know her as well as we thought we did.

D observes C.

F You're doing well!

C See how fascinating it is. See what we reveal about ourselves? What simple creatures. How we move in simple behavioural patterns. Like those of a hand-made quilt. How easy it is to spot the anomalous, wonky lines, the wonky behaviour. You look at what you've got, sort the wheat from the chaff and then bring it to harvest. (*Pause.*) And then sell it at the market. Right now we're at the market. I'm selling my analysis. And I'm charging ten points. Not five, not six, ten points. *Ten* to help you find the watch.

F But there is no crime.

D points at C, accusingly.

D Her face!

F Not since I have lived here.

C There's always ill doing.

F No crime.

Pause.

C My watch is missing.

F –

C Someone has stolen my timepiece. Help. Help. What are you going to do about it?

THIRTY-ONE

A, B, C, D, E and F
C looks closely at the five quilts. She lights a candle to inspect them with.

D No one stole her watch because –

C It's patterns within patterns. Interesting, very interesting.

B It's just quilts.

C That's why you need an expert.

B I don't remember a watch.

D . . . Because there *are* no watches.

C examines a quilt, addresses B.

C Is this one yours?

B panics.

B What?

C A moment . . .

B What can you see?

C It's OK . . .

She examines another black quilt.

Interesting . . . Whose is this? The stitching here is tentative. And there are mistakes and the sewer has gone back over this section repeatedly. As if hiding something.

This section looks like it was sewn at four a.m. A very strange time to be sewing. Abnormally late. And the colour of the thread is slightly off. It's almost right but not quite as it should be. Not totally normal.

I'm picking up on funny little details. Odd little details.

And of course the grass stains.

And the mud stains. It doesn't look like she's a regular grass-stainer. Just this once. Odd.

I think it's you. OK?

C points to D.

It's her.

F Keep going.

D She's not pretending.

A She is.

C I think the punishment is that we don't even give you a chance to respond. Just take her away. OK?

A She ought to have a hearing of some sort.

E A hearing?

C A hearing, right here. OK.

D Is this in scenario?

C goes into D's sewing bundle. She pulls out a flashy watch.

B We don't know what that is.

A It's a timepiece of some kind?

C This is vintage rose-gold Rolex, 18 carat, rectangular with full Arabic numeral dial, blue steel hands, mechanical movement.

F Remember the scenario.

A I can't.

C There's no point in just making quilts. They have to serve the village. They have to *do* something. This is what they do.

A They keep us warm.

C Warm at night, leads to good sleep, leads to good productivity, leads to expression of self, leads to reveal of self, leads to collection of that information, leads to a safer, more just world through – quilt-analysis. OK.

A Quilts.

C You can't embroider lace for ever, OK. You have to ask, 'What's next?'

B Did she steal a watch or –?

A We should be asking, 'What's a watch?'

E There is a watch. Right there.

C I don't understand what's wrong. This is a logical progression.

D I can't tell if this is real or not.

C You're pulling us backwards. OK.

F Hold your arcs. Stay in scenario!

C Why won't you move forward? OK.

F You're bunching.

C I CAN SPOT PATTERNS IN THE MOTHERFUCKING QUILTS. IT'S IN THE FUCKING THREADS YOU FUCKING

44

BACKWARD FUCKING PEASANTS. THIS IS BASIC DATA ANALYTICS. JUST READ THE FUCKING STITCHES AND GET THE FUCK OUT OF MY FACES. IF YOU DON'T PUNISH HER I FUCKING WILL. I HAVE THE BALLS I CAN DO IT FOR YOU.

C reaches for the scissors. F takes them before her. He has them in his hand. The others back away.

OK.

D She hasn't been in scenario since the embroidery.

D starts to pile the quilts.

F Stay in it!

D We finished, she made us start again. We're making quilts and you're holding scissors. Watches exist. She's a 'quilt analyst'. I don't like it. We can't just sew, we have to reveal information about ourselves, to be used against us. She's ruined sewing. It's supposed to be 'idyllic' and 'sparse'. She's a computer person?

Pause.

Isn't she?!

C I'm a sewer.

The others gather round D.

A Your husband's not working.

B You've got a daughter.

E Watch after your job.

A Forget about it.

E You should just stay in scenario.

D We're not *actually* peasant women, you know!

C We *have* to stay in scenario? Isn't that the rule?

45

F Did you steal it?

D ignores F, takes the candle and holds it to the pile of quilts.

C She can't just set us on fire?

F Shit, Sally.

A takes the scissors from F, and leaves.

C We'll make new quilts. We'll make back-up quilts next time.

D says something inaudible.

What did she say? What did you say?

D shakes her head. Full of disdain.
E approaches D.
D whispers to E.

What's she saying?

E She says if you were acting we'd know, because you'd have to be telling the truth.

C So much fucking bullshit. Make the fucking quilts like I said or fuck yourselves off. Fuck yourselves off!

They back away and stare at her.
A returns with a fire-extinguisher and puts it all out.
Silence.

THIRTY-TWO

D gets changed into her jeans, watching from the side.
C sits alone sewing. E sits next to her.

E OK?

C Yes.

E You're a bit alone now.

C Yep.

E It's not what you wanted.

C Nope.

E You wanted to be surrounded by good people.

C Yep.

E You wanted to be part of a community.

C Yep.

E You wanted to rediscover your soul. The old Maggie.

C Did I say that?

E You wanted to sew something nice.

C Improve team work.

E Push.

C Screen break.

E Even me, your 'aunt'. Pushed away.

C Have I?

E You have closed your heart to what is good.

C Have I though?

E Look. (*Pause.*) The others are afraid of you.

   D starts eating a sandwich from a foil package.

C Did I get a ten?

E We're still '*here*'.

C Maybe it's because you don't know how bad things could get without me. You're just like some of our clients.

E The winter's coming.

C She stole a watch. Guess what comes next?

E No watches commonplace for a hundred years.

C She stole your bank account details, she stole movement of troops, she stole two people emailing each other about making a bomb to blow up your house.

Pause.

I didn't mean to upset anyone.

F comes in.
C is instantly irritated by him.

F There must be a dozen dragonflies by the meadow this morning.

Silence.

C Sorry, no.

She tries to get out of the dress, but the buttons are fiddly. We see some of her sleek office wear underneath.
She becomes frustrated.
F tries to help.

I said at the beginning no contact. I ticked that box on the form. Don't touch me. I think we've taken this as far as it can go. I think . . . that's it now. OK. Well . . . OK . . . (*Slightly desperate.*) how long have I even been in here?! I've got work to do.

She can't unbutton the dress.
She becomes exasperated.
F hugs her.

F It's going to be alright. You've done really well.

C I'm a bit shaken.

F Yes, yes. Well done. Well done.

C leans into him.

C It's tiring.

F I know, I know. There, there.

C I did really well.

F That's OK.

C I need a ten now.

F You're OK, you're OK.

C I didn't expect it to be like this. I shouldn't have said yes to doing this. I've got too much going on. The past really isn't of much interest to me. I like my life. What time is it?

> *She relaxes into the hug for a moment.*
> *He soothes her.*
> *He smoothes her hair.*

F I need to let you know before we come out of the scenario, while we are very, very calm, that we'll need to bring your mark down. (*Pause.*) Three's the new ceiling.

> *Pause.*

I know how hard you tried. But by way of the swearing and the aggression and the demeaning attitude towards my team.

C I'm a ten. Always.

F My hands are tied.

> *She twists up in his arms.*

C I'm the scorer. You don't score me. I score you.

F We need to bring you down to a three.

C There is no three. One, two, four, five, six, seven, eight, nine, ten.

*He gets accidentally tangled with her as she tries to
get away.*

She struggles.

*The others, except D who is just watching, come
back in. They are in a kind of T-shirt and leggings
now. One or two T-shirts have a logo on them.*

C pushes F to the ground.

He clings on to her dress.

C panics and punches him. Then falls on to him.

F END! END! You fucking-nutjob-bitch-motherfucker.
That's it.

The others (except D) pull C off F.

F raises his hand. Gives a signal.

'End of the journey' orchestral music plays.

*The lighting opens out. The 'room' is revealed to
be actually a studio box dressed with wood, with
freestanding lights lighting it from all around.*

*The box sits in a much wider basement space of a
commercial office building.*

A box of blossom.

A props box.

F is holding his nose.

C realises it's ending.

C Don't stop yet. Please.

A crouches next to C, in professional mode.

A We only have five minutes left with you and we think
the session needs to 'wrap up' now.

F This shit-show stops. Your company might pay a
fuckload but it's not enough.

C You're supposed to be running a 'hold all' set up.

F I think you found the chink.

C You get paid so we can 'go on a journey', don't you? What about my arc? My arc matters.

F You wait until you see all the extra charges. *Your* arc's expensive.

C looks around her indicating the expensive building above.

C How ever will we international-mega-corporation-afford-it? I thought you ran journeys for the Cabinet.

F Shadow.

C And?

F We haven't done computer people before.

C What's the difference?

F Believe it or not, *they* don't think they're masters of the universe. They really don't.

C There's stuff I wanted to get to. There's other stuff. My arc. Isn't it?

Pause.

I apologise. I'm dehydrated. I haven't done it the way we wanted me to. I haven't hit my outcome. I'm a three, you're right, I'm sorry. I didn't play it straight. I fell back into old habits. I didn't get into it properly. I was slipping in and out all the time. I'm not actor. I didn't just sew and be nice and discover something small and meaningful. I should have done that. There's so much to improve. There's so much history can teach us. I hold my hands up. Please. I want to do it once more. The way it should be. I'm OK to be in the past. I can go there now. More blossom. Less quilt. I promise.

She grabs A and B.

Just us three.

C And you two, take a break for me over there.
(*Meaning E and F.*)

F I'm running this. Let's move, people.

C One more go!

E I know we're not supposed to know. But I did some reading while I was 'off'. Their company does important work. They help the government stop terrorists. They do the computer work. Don't you?

C I'm not allowed to say.

E It's not an easy thing to do.

C I couldn't confirm.

E If she wants blossom for five minutes . . .

C Thank you.

F What we do is create simple pathways in very simple scenarios. She agreed to sit and sew and chat for a few hours to see what comes to the surface. She refused to play along. We spent ages on her arc before we even touched a needle and thread; a teen in trouble looking for redemption. She's taken over our arc. She's stolen your arcs. Miss Computer Engineer is not the author of the 'world' in here. We are.

E I feel sorry for her. This whole place gives me the creeps. What does it matter? At the end of the day, we walk out of here and we're these free people. More than that, we're actors.

C studies E, wounded and also surprised at her naivety.

C Exactly.

Pause.

F All this cleared!

C Ready, you two?

A and B half pull their dresses back on.
Their costumes look half-arsed.

Good energy!

She clicks at the hidden lighting desk.
The lighting resumes.

Blossom!

E dumps the box of blossom on the floor.

Breeze!

D sets up a fan; it blows the blossom.
C whispers to A and B.

What's his name? His real name.

A Alec Davidson.

C Where's he from?

A I don't know. Watford?

C Oh. (*Pause.*) You're my daughters now. In this bit.
You call me Mummy.

They squirm, unwilling.
C takes a fifty-quid note from under her dress, she
gives it to them. B takes it.

B We need a moment to . . .

C waits.

Yes. OK.

THIRTY-THREE

Idyllic lighting, a perfect scene. Bird sounds.
  C enters. She's acting serene.
  A and B join in, they do their best to follow her lead.

A Oh hi, Mum.

C *Mummy.*

A Mummy! You're here!

B Mummy finally!

C Hello, children.

A Where have you been?

C I have been walking along the river and it was so beautiful, and I saw old Mrs . . . Julipple.

B Old Mrs Julipple?

C Julipple, yes. And she looked so old and cold.

A She *is* always complaining of the cold.

C I want us to make her a very simple plain blanket. As a gift from the kindness of our hearts. We won't even charge for materials.

  They start to thread their needles.

A grey one. Just very, very simple with a bit of ribbon trim. No ribbon trim! Just the very simple blanket and it doesn't matter if it is wonky. It *should* look homespun. It should just be full of love and that's all that matters. Will you help me?

A Yes, Mamma.

C You're like this. And I'm like this. And . . .

  They sew.

C starts singing, shakily at first. And then an old folk song she didn't know she remembered.

'Mid pleasures and palaces though we may roam,
Be it ever so humble, there's no place like home;
A charm from the sky seems to hallow us there,
Which, seek through the world, is ne'er met with
    elsewhere.

Home, home! Sweet, sweet home!
There's no place like home.
There's no place like home.

A Really good singing.

B We love you, Mamma.

C And your little faces! How many cheese strings have you had today?

B One!

A Two each.

B Let's be together.

A Let's watch *Peppa Pig*.

C It's wonderful to be here, you are so little. You grow up so fast. I'm always chasing after –

A Leaves?

C Leaves?

A You can't chase leaves all day every day.

C Well, I get very caught up. You do actually have to keep up. Everything moves incredibly fast. We can't keep up!

B Do we live here now, by the river?

A We can tell Daddy we live here now.

Silence.

D comes closer, watches with the others.

C You can't live here. It's just a holiday rental.

B Where do we live?

A Where do you live?

C It must be very confusing for you. I knew I was going to reach a point at the end of the project, wasn't I? And then there was the next project wasn't there, and there isn't time to even sleep or breathe when that's happening. And Mummy was going to sort it all out, it was on my list to have a proper sit-down.

B We can start again.

C Well, hardly, well, perhaps if I could travel back in time!

A You should make us a time machine.

C Don't be silly.

B Time ma-chine!

A Time ma-chine!

C I actually said *if* I could travel back in time.

B *If.*

C Yes. Maybe, if OK, *if* I had a time machine, which is silly but! I could go back to, um, to before anyone got as clever, before computer engineers, before machines, before the industrial revolution which you haven't learned about yet, but you will, all of that, anyway, then I'd be able to do things differently. To before we made decisions that have got us to where we are now . . . Yeah, maybe then we could start it all again.

B Same.

A It would be the same all over again, Mummy.

C I don't know. (*Pause.*) It wouldn't.

B How do you know?

C It wouldn't be the same.

A Would we be the same?

C Yes. You would be the same.

A Would you be the same?

Pause.

C Of course.

B Would you still have us?

C looks at D, unsure how to respond.
D enters the scenario. She inhabits the role of C's ex-husband without seeming to do anything to make it happen. It's just as if she's him.

D Are they ready to go?

C You're early.

D The traffic wasn't as bad as I thought.

C How are things?

D Fine.

C Does everything work at the new house?

D thinks . . .

D Yep, the boiler's a bit sticky, but apart from that.

C If you need any money. On top of . . .

D Yeah, no, we're OK.

C There are some big things happening at work. It's exciting. This next development –

D Great.

C Honestly, some of the software we're working on, it can do stuff you never even –

D I don't want to hit the traffic on the way back.

C OK.

D Have they eaten?

Silence.

C Did you talk to them about the . . . new school?

D Yes.

Pause.

C What did you say?

D I don't remember.

C Roughly?

D Well . . . I reassured them. I told them it's all going to be OK.

C Like what?

D Just . . . we're still a family.

C OK?

D Yeah.

C Like what?

D Yeah.

C Like what?

D Birthdays and Christmases.

C Oh.

D I made something up.

C Oh fuck off.

Pause.

D You talk to them then.

C I'll skype them in the week –

D You never do, but that's OK.

C When I'm on an international project like this with all the time zones it's actually very, but the next one is less –

D Girls, let's go.

C I wouldn't be doing all of this, if I didn't genuinely believe in –

D Great.

C (*almost inaudibly*) This is the Silicon Revolution. It's 'the Renaissance two'.

D Is it.

A long pause.

D That's right.

A Bye, Mummy.

B –

C Be good for your dad in the car.

They go.

Wait! I want to . . . (*To D.*) I know you think I always get upset but then I just re-boot or . . . you think *I'm* the machine! I should have said a bit more? I should have done that a bit better, shouldn't I? I didn't know what to say.

D doesn't respond.

What?

Unwillingly, C cries now for real? A release.
  D puts 'his' hand on her shoulder, reassuringly.
  C starts taking off her black costume dress.
  She's wearing low-key office clothes underneath.

59

C (*exhausted*) That's it. Thank you, everyone.

The rest of the team come in, one of them has a T-shirt that says 'Simpler Times' on it.
They start packing up, in silence.
The lighting changes to low 'normal state'.
A digital countdown clock can be seen. It shows two minutes, then begins counting backwards.
Someone puts a foil blanket over C's shoulders, like she's just done a marathon.
She's brought a bottle of water.
B brings an electronic box and a plastic pen.

B Sign here to say you received your employee day Simpler Times real-life re-enactment adventure. 'No computers, no tech, just real-life people'. No harm was done to your person, reputation or physical being during this activity?

F is bleeding from the nose. C grabs his arm.

C Alec?

F looks around for cameras, suddenly afraid they're being watched

Alec Davidson.

Pause.

Alec Davidson from Watford? What's the mark?

F The mark doesn't matter you know. The company pay for the experience, but they don't own it. The mark is just for you. This is what *we* call a 'safe space'.

C –

F 'One hundred guaranteed'. That's on our website. We usually gather and thank each other for a moment at the end. Whatever happens while you're in here is between all of us. A lot of people find that very liberating.

He sighs.

Ten. (*Pause.*) For when you . . . for the . . . (*He indicates tears.*)

He walks towards the exit holding his bloody nose.
He stops, returns to the centre, looks up again into
the lights.

If you find the cue. Just take it.

F exits.

B Here.

Maggie signs.
A phone on the wall rings.
E answers it.

E Got a call here for Exec VP Maggie O'Sullivan. You're needed upstairs in the Big Ideas soft room, for video conference with the Beijing office.

C I have two more minutes, don't I? Where's my phone?

A No phones until 'time up'. You need to give back the costume, start moving out. The next client arrives right on the dot.

C Give me your phone.

A No can do.

C clutches her chest.
She waits, abandoned for a moment.
D gives her her mobile instead.

D Here.

C takes it, grateful.
D helps her unbutton her dress.

C (*at A*) Fifty quid and you'll get on your knees, pretend you're a five-year-old. That's twenty-five between two! Incredible. (*Pause.*) They're in their teens now!

She struggles to breathe normally.
She makes the call. It goes to voicemail.

It's Mummy. I just wanted to call because . . . I wanted to make time to . . . to say I'm . . .

Sorry we haven't spoken for so long. I'm always thinking about you . . .

OK? . . .

The dress hangs off her knees now.
C struggles to ride the wave of new emotions.
Everyone stops to calmly listen to her call.
She moves to a different spot, to be more private,
but it isn't.

Um . . .

Pause.

. . . I'm sorry I didn't make it out to your birthdays last month. There was a big internal software launch here, same day! I had to be here to . . . I hope you both had a lovely time. I wish I could have . . .

Pause.

Same day we launched . . . It was a really significant . . . I remember . . . It was . . . I know it will make a massive difference to . . . It was an industry milestone! I remember that! It was definitely a big one. It was only a month ago . . . (*Pause.*) I just can't remember . . . what we made.

Silence.

Say hi to your dad from me . . .

Pause.

I love you.

Pause.

I'm incredibly lucky to get to be part of all of this. These are incredibly exciting times!

She stays on the line a moment.
  Hangs up.
  C hands the phone back to D. D takes it.
  C steps out of her dress, leaving it like a black puddle on the floor.
  C is handed and drinks her espresso.
  The clock counts to near zero.
  B brings her a plastic box with her personal effects in it.
  C puts on her jacket.
  Her shoes.
  Her company pass.
  Takes her phone.
  The wooden set is packed up around her.
  Two lift doors open.
  An exec, Mac, in a low-key suit steps out. He sees Maggie.

Mac Hey! *So*, how was your 'employee journey experience'?

Maggie Oh, you know . . .
  Fun! Mac: fun!

Mac laughs.

Mac What mark?

Maggie Ten! Mac: ten!

She tries a modest grin.

There was a moment during the . . . where I . . . (*Pause.*) And then I realised, if in this day and age, you were looking for an example of a . . . ten . . .

  Pause.

Mac You OK, Maggie? You me still going to get that juice sometime soon?

Maggie Well, Mac. So . . . what's yours?

Mac Oh! Cowboys and Indians.

Maggie –

Mac It's to do with 'saying yes to . . .' Um? I forget.

Maggie Horses?

Mac Yeah. Or 'wildness' or something. I told them I want to work on not being *too* efficient and reliable. We agreed my objective should be 'learn how to be more spontaneous'.

He mimes shooting out of a holster like a cowboy.

Maggie You're working on the big national security project –

Mac Shh! (*Quickly switching subject.*) You never do these things.

Maggie struggles to retain composure.

Maggie We agreed I wanted to work on 'trusting people . . . in new teams', and . . . 'timeline review'.

Pause.

They gave me a Sewing Group in the seventeen hundreds. I had to pretend to be a sort of younger person, lost? Who had to sew all the time. Because that's all there was for people then, at that time. They got all hunched over and their fingers . . . all . . .
   Whatever it is . . .
   She was supposed to . . .
   Have done . . .
   No one would care now.
   Um . . . Because you can do anything. No one cares.

She holds up her sewing pouch to show him.

Mac The company certainly likes to go all out. All these actual people. No screens! They're really looking after us. Expensive.

Long pause.

The seventeen hundreds? I can't even imagine . . . What a time? What an interesting . . . What a real time to be alive. What a real time. What a real time to be alive? Really . . .

Maggie, do you ever get headaches? Right here.

He presses on the centre of his forehead.
Maggie recognises exactly what he's saying. She touches her head.

If we don't like it, we just say we want a different experience next year!

He goes over to the cowboy set, takes out a replica pistol.
E approaches Maggie.
The rest of the group gather, hold hands a moment, and murmur thanks to each other.

E Mrs Sullivan? We're missing a sewing pouch.

Maggie I forgot.

Maggie returns it reluctantly.

E Your 'Simpler Times' experience is now over!

The lighting cue finds its moment. It widens out once more to reveal the depth of the room and the reality of the office block basement; a fire hose, an exit sign.
The 'set change' whirls around her.
Mac wrestles with a pair of chaps.
Cowboy hats emerge.
Blossom swirls in the air.
A few black dresses still left out.

The past looks beautiful.

The clock counter resets to zero.

Mac loads fake ammunition into the replica gun.

Maggie sweeps her hair back and straightens her jacket.

She checks her make-up in the steel reflection.

The lift arrives like a time machine. The doors open. A terrifying 'ding' sound.

The others stop working for a moment and look at her.

Maggie puts her hand up, to say goodbye.

Black.

Selected References

Susan Greenfield, *Mind Change: How Digital Technologies are Leaving their Mark on our Brains* (Rider Books, 2014).

Lewis Mumford, *Technics and Civilization* (University of Chicago Press, reprint, 2010).

Steven Levy, *In the Plex: How Google Thinks, Works and Shapes Our Lives* (Simon and Schuster, 2011).

'How a "Deviant" Philosopher built Palantir, a CIA-Funded Data-mining Juggernaut', *Forbes*, 3 September 2013.